Table of Contents

Global Connections

There are almost eight billion people on Earth. That's a lot of humans across one planet! Around the globe, each of these people is living a unique life. But we all have a lot in common, too.

Everyone is a part of their local community. This is your home. It's where you live and learn. We often take active roles in our communities. Many of us will find ways to care for our homes. You may pick up trash in your neighborhood. A friend might volunteer at a food bank. All these actions add up to a healthy home.

Citizens of Planet Earth

Monika Davies

Reader Consultants

Brian Allman, M.A.
Classroom Teacher, West Virginia

Cynthia Donovan
Classroom Teacher, California

iCivics Consultants

Emma Humphries, Ph.D.
Chief Education Officer

Taylor Davis, M.T.
Director of Curriculum and Content

Natacha Scott, MAT
Director of Educator Engagement

Publishing Credits

Rachelle Cracchiolo, M.S.Ed., *Publisher*
Emily R. Smith, M.A.Ed., *VP of Content Development*
Véronique Bos, *Creative Director*
Dona Herweck Rice, *Senior Content Manager*
Dani Neiley, *Associate Editor*
Fabiola Sepulveda, *Series Designer*
Jessica Liu, *Illustrator, pages 6–9*

Image Credits: p5 Shutterstock/Parikh Mahendra N; p11 Alamy/Mark Boulton; p19 Courtesy of Food for Education; p21 Library of Congress [LC-USZ62-31799]; p22 Newscom/Kyodo; p26 Courtesy Elia Saikaly; p28 Shutterstock/Anirut Thailand; all other images from iStock and/or Shutterstock

Library of Congress Cataloging-in-Publication Data

Names: Davies, Monika, author.
Title: Citizens of planet earth / Monika Davies.
Other titles: ICivics (Teacher Created Materials, Inc.)
Description: Huntington Beach, CA : Teacher Created Materials, [2022] | Includes index. | Audience: Grades 4-6 | Summary: "Our worldwide community is facing numerous challenges. However, there are many ways we can help out! As global citizens, we can start by learning more about our world. We can also fight for issues affecting people around the globe. Let's look at some of our global challenges-and learn how we can each lend a hand"-- Provided by publisher.
Identifiers: LCCN 2021045463 (print) | LCCN 2021045464 (ebook) | ISBN 9781087615424 (Paperback) | ISBN 9781087628837 (ePub)
Subjects: LCSH: World citizenship--Juvenile literature. | Social change--Juvenile literature. | Child volunteers--Juvenile literature.
Classification: LCC JZ1320.4 .D38 2022 (print) | LCC JZ1320.4 (ebook) | DDC 323.6--dc23/eng/20211105
LC record available at https://lccn.loc.gov/2021045463
LC ebook record available at https://lccn.loc.gov/2021045464

TCM Teacher Created Materials
5482 Argosy Avenue
Huntington Beach, CA 92649
www.tcmpub.com

ISBN 978-1-0876-1542-4

Printed by: 590835
Printed in: China

But we are also all part of a larger community. Every person shares the same home: planet Earth. Since we share a home, we are part of the same worldwide community.

Our global community faces many challenges. And there are ways we can help out. We can each begin by becoming a global citizen. Global citizens learn about their world. They work for issues affecting people worldwide. Caring about their home is important to them. And they know that we are all in this together.

Jump into Fiction

Kira and Dad in Vietnam

Kira had never left America before. But she and her dad always took an annual summer trip. And this time, Dad was taking Kira to Vietnam! He wanted her to learn more about where his family had come from.

The two arrived in Hanoi. For Kira, everything looked, tasted, and felt different from what she was used to. Her eyes spun in circles, trying to keep track of everything new. Thousands of scooters streamed down the streets. Street vendors crowded the sidewalks.

"Everything is so different here, huh?" Kira said to her dad. He just smiled at her.

A week later, they traveled down to Hoi An. On their first day, they went on a bike tour around the city. Halfway through, the group came across an older woman. She was using long, skinny blades of grass to make a mat. Their guide said, "She weaves these mats, day in and day out. It's a lot of work. However, a weaver makes just about two dollars a day."

Kira felt her heart squeeze. She remembered her dad had paid $45 each for their bike tour. The woman weaving the mats looked right at Kira. She nodded her head and smiled. Kira smiled back, feeling very shy.

That evening, Kira and her dad sat on little plastic stools by the city's river. They ordered their dinner off a simple menu with very low prices.

"What did you think about the bike tour?" Dad asked.

"It was lots of fun…but it was tough seeing the weaver making mats. I've never really thought about the ways that life might be different for people around the world."

Dad nodded his head thoughtfully. "At home, we talk a lot about what it means to be an American citizen. We have rights and responsibilities. But we should also keep in mind that we're global citizens."

"What's that?"

"It means we're citizens of a worldwide community," Dad replied. "Our family…well, we're lucky that we have the money for all our needs as well as to travel. You can go to school at no cost. But others around the world don't always have the same opportunities." He thought for a minute and added, "Being a global citizen means being aware of the world around us. It also means working with others to build a world that is equal and fair."

Kira blinked, thinking about her dad's words. "How do we do that?" she asked.

Dad smiled and put his arm around Kira's shoulders. "We can start by getting curious. Staying open-minded helps us learn how to walk in another's shoes. And that's often when real change starts."

Back to Nonfiction

Becoming Active Citizens

Our global community is huge. It is also **diverse**. Day to day, we might stay focused on our local surroundings. But we also need a wider **viewpoint**. There are many shared worldwide challenges. Large groups of people face these issues. Addressing them is our work as global citizens.

Think and Talk

What effect can a drought have on our global community?

Simple changes like this can help reduce water waste.

Looking at our role in the world is the first place to start. Every day, we make choices. All these choices carry an impact. Our choices affect us—and the people around us. Global citizens choose actions that will help others. Their choices keep in mind that there are billions of people worldwide. And everyone matters.

Global citizens also work with others. As a team, they help solve global issues. One of their goals is a fair future for people across the planet. They stay hopeful that we can all make change happen.

The great news is that everyone can become an active global citizen! And it's not so hard to do.

Stay Curious

Global citizens love to learn. They like to meet new people. Their meals include food from other cultures. New languages intrigue them. And they stay open-minded. New ideas are seen as useful. They actively listen to others. If they don't know about a global topic, they research it. This is how they stay open to change.

People have different beliefs. Someone may lead a very different life from you. But you can learn something new from anyone. Staying curious helps us grow. A curious mindset is key to being a global citizen.

Know Your Values

What is important to you? Do you value lovc and family? Perhaps you also value service for others. Values are things that are important to you. Your list of values is your own. They guide how you live your life.

Global citizens share many values. Equity is one of them. They believe everyone should be treated fairly. Respect for others is also key. They work to see beyond differences.

Valuing Diversity

Someone's skin color may be different from yours. You might not agree with someone's beliefs. But global citizens value diversity. They believe that different perspectives can help solve issues. This is important for facing global challenges.

Build Empathy

Empathy is a core trait of global citizens. It means to see and think about another's experiences. This can take practice. Using empathy, we can "walk in another's shoes." Understanding the pain of others leads us to think about change. This also moves us toward creating a fair future for all.

Working together is an easy and natural way to build empathy.

Believe in the Future

A global citizen knows they can make a difference. Some global issues may seem tough to solve. It can be hard to hold onto hope. But change can still happen.

A global citizen sees their power. They know that many of their choices can have a global impact. Everyone can take action. For instance, speaking up about global issues is one way to use your voice. We can all take small steps to make change happen. Working together on issues is how we build a brighter future for our planet.

So, these are ways to become an active global citizen. Next up is learning what some of the global issues are—and how to help.

Giving Back

Have you ever thought about volunteering at a food bank? A food bank is a place where people who don't have enough to eat can pick up food for free. Donating to and volunteering at a food bank is one way to give back to your community.

Enough Food for All

Every human being needs food to live. It's key for our survival. The human body needs nutrients to grow strong. Yet, every day, over 820 million people worldwide go to bed hungry. This is a major global issue. And it's a challenge for global citizens to solve.

Unequal Food Systems

Our global food system is not equal. It's not set up so everyone has access to enough food. People who are hungry are often too poor to buy food. They are also unlikely to have the resources to grow their own food. Sadly, hunger continues the cycle of hunger. Someone who is hungry has less energy. It becomes harder for them to meet their needs. They are then less likely to learn and find work.

Creating a world without hunger is **complex**. Big steps are needed to create global change. Some of these big steps have to come from higher levels. This might be new government policies. But being a global citizen means everyone can take action. You can also take small steps to help out.

A Growing Population

Researchers believe Earth's population will keep growing. It is **projected** that by 2050, there will be over nine billion people on the planet. That means there will be one billion more mouths to feed!

A big issue facing us is food waste. This happens when we throw out food someone else could eat. Around 30 to 40 percent of U.S. food supply is food waste! You can help your family take steps to reduce food waste. Plan grocery lists with meals in mind. Unused cans can be donated to a food bank. Ask your family to **compost** food scraps.

As global citizens, we can also learn more about the benefits of food. Knowing the importance of food is key to our health. Sharing that knowledge can help build healthy communities.

Think and Talk

How can food waste affect the global community?

A Global Citizen in Action

Wawira Njiru knows food is crucial. She's the founder of Food for Education. Growing up in Kenya, she saw a lot of people suffer from hunger. She also saw a link between health and education. This led to the creation of her company. It provides meals to students. Many students now have access to healthy food. She believes "young people can lead the way in bringing change."

Wawira Njiru

Shokuiku

In Japan, students help serve and prepare the lunches at school. Food education (*shokuiku* in Japanese) is important to them. They learn about the nutrition behind their meals. Lunchtime is never rushed in Japan's schools. This highlights the importance of food for a healthy body and mind!

Equal Opportunities for All

Girls and women equal half of our global community. Yet some of them struggle to have the same freedoms as boys and men. This is seen in many systems. Women have less access to schooling than men. Women are also more likely to face **violence**.

In many countries, steps have been made for women's rights. Women in the United States have the right to vote. They can own property. And women also can take part in government. But these freedoms are not shared by all women across the world. Remember: global citizens value equality. So, how can we make sure everyone has the same freedoms?

How Can You Help?

Start by learning about **gender discrimination**. For instance, many women work for a living. But they often face unequal treatment. Some women earn less than men who do the same job. They may have less support in their workplace. Many women are also **harassed** on the job.

Research some struggles that are specific to women. Then, you can discuss these issues with others. Raising awareness is key. This helps prompt change.

More Than Gender

Gender is just one area in which people often do not have equal opportunities. Race, economic status, ability, and more are big issues. People around the world are constantly at work to bring equal opportunities for all.

You can also support women in your own life. Encourage them to dream big. Support women so they can reach their goals. Every girl is full of potential. As global citizens, we can help **empower** the women of tomorrow.

A Global Citizen in Action

Malala Yousafzai has a strong voice. She grew up in Pakistan. When she was young, a military group seized control over her hometown. The group declared girls could not go to school. Yousafzai deeply loved going to school. In protest, she began speaking up about girls' right to learn. Her voice for women's rights made her a target. In 2012, a gunman shot her in the head. Luckily, she survived the attack.

She kept speaking up. Her voice is now heard on a global stage. In 2013, she put together the Malala Fund. Her charity promotes girls' education. The goal is to make sure more girls' stories are heard. By sharing stories, she creates space for girls' voices to be heard.

Malala Yousafzai

Unequal Statistics

Worldwide, women earn about 23 percent less than men do for the same work. Only about one-third of government seats belong to women. And women do two to three times more unpaid household work, such as caring for children and cleaning, than men do.

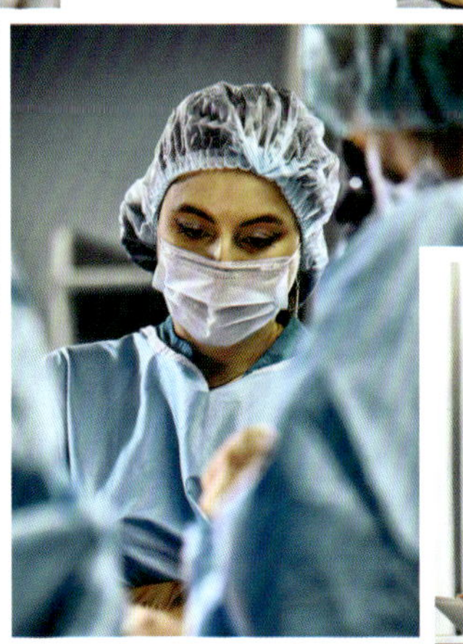

A Healthy Planet for All

As global citizens, we need to take care of our planet. Climate change is a vital topic. Over the last one hundred years, Earth's surface has warmed up. This has led to many worrying effects. Earth's sea levels are rising. Our planet's glaciers are melting. And Earth's temperatures are going up. This is known as *global warming*.

Global climate change is a challenge to Earth's future. Experts tell us that it is mainly due to human activities. We burn fossil fuels, such as coal or gas. These fuels create carbon dioxide. This is a greenhouse gas. Carbon dioxide stays in our atmosphere. It lingers for a long period of time. This causes the greenhouse effect. Earth is growing warmer as a result.

How Can You Help?

Climate change is at a crucial point. A lot of help is needed to make sure our planet has a healthy future. Big steps are needed from our leaders. The fight against climate change has to start now and needs to be a **priority**.

But there are still small steps everyone can take. Every global citizen can speak up about climate change. When we speak up, we can **unite** to create change. Industries and governments must shift practices to fight global warming. By raising our voices, we can drive leaders to take action.

Fewer Trees, More CO_2

Across the planet, more and more trees have been cut down. This usually is to make space for new buildings or farmland. Trees are necessary to absorb carbon dioxide (CO_2). Removing them adds to the greenhouse effect.

You can also make changes in your own life. Choosing to walk or bike instead of driving helps our planet. You can plant trees in your local area.

There are many small steps we can all take. And making changes can also inspire those around us! When we make steps toward positive change, this encourages others to make changes, too.

A Global Citizen in Action

Elia Saikaly

Elia Saikaly is passionate about inspiring people. He wants to bring people together to make the world a better place.

Saikaly is an adventurer. He travels the world, climbing mountains and exploring. He is also a filmmaker. He films places and people around the world. He uses his films to inspire others to "live their most meaningful life" and "to spark positive change."

One way Saikaly does these things is through working with **charities**. He brings attention to their causes. He also works with children around the world to raise money to help others. They use the money to build needed things, such as schools and wells.

Saikaly has traveled a lot. He has learned about life around the world. He sees firsthand the help that is needed. Now, it's his mission to shine a light on what people can do to help one another.

Less Meat

Research suggests that eating less meat is a way to fight climate change. Often, forests are cut down to make room for **livestock**. The animals also release greenhouse gases into the atmosphere. To help the issue, families might choose to eat one or two meals each week without meat.

Reaching Out

Our world is home to billions of people. We live a great distance from most of them. But we are all connected. Suffering for some is suffering for all.

People come from all walks of life. We all have our own stories to tell. But everyone needs food to eat. Everyone loves. And everyone has a wish not to suffer. As global citizens, we can make that wish our worldwide goal.

Every day, try looking for small ways to make a difference. Read a book about another country. Check out a world map, and think about what life is like for someone very far from you. Research new ideas online. Talk to someone you don't know very well. Look for chances to volunteer in your community. These small steps are how we become active and responsible global citizens.

We are facing many global challenges. Remembering to stay hopeful and on the lookout for ways to work together is key. Building lasting change will take time. It will also take a lot of hard work. But global citizens are up to the task!

Glossary

charities—organizations that help people who are in need

complex—having parts that connect or go together in complicated ways

compost—to change into a decayed mixture of plants that is used to improve the soil in a garden

discrimination—the practice of unfairly treating a person or group of people differently from other people or groups of people

diverse—different from each other

empower—to give power to someone

gender—related to a person's sex, such as male or female

harassed—annoyed or bothered someone in a constant or repeated way

livestock—farm animals that are kept, raised, and used by people

priority—something that is more important than other things and that needs to be done or dealt with first

projected—estimated for the future

unite—to join together to do or achieve something

viewpoint—a way of looking at or thinking about something

violence—the use of physical force to harm someone, to damage property, etc.

Index

Civics in Action

Global citizens educate themselves. Then, they take action. You can be a global citizen right now! It's as easy as one, two, three, four.

1. As a class, choose an issue in your community that you can help. What need does the community have that isn't being met?

2. Find out about the issue. Who does it affect? What are the consequences of it? What has been done in the past to fix it?

3. Brainstorm things your community can do to help the issue.

4. Write a class letter to a community leader. Tell them about the problem and what you think should be done. Send your letter!